The Onion You Are Eating Is Someone Else's Water Lily

By

Bernice Gorham Cherry

© 2004 by Bernice Gorham Cherry. All rights reserved.

No part of this book may be reproduced, stored in a retrieval system, or transmitted by any means, electronic, mechanical, photocopying, recording, or otherwise, without written permission from the author.

ISBN: 1-4140-3621-3 (e-book)
ISBN: 1-4140-3620-5 (Paperback)

Library of Congress Control Number: 2003098665

This book is printed on acid free paper.

Printed in the United States of America
Bloomington, IN

Scripture quotations are from the King James Version of the Bible.

1stBooks - rev. 1/19/04

Acknowledgements

To my church family at Faith & Victory Church – this was not just my victory it was your victory as well. Thank you for walking this journey with us in prayer, service and love.

To my church family at Sandy Branch Baptist Church – thank you for your prayers.

To Dr. Jeffrey Hoggard and Eastern Nephrology Associates – thank you for your relentless efforts to save my life.

To my circle of sisters – thank you for standing together in the gap as prayer warriors, cooks, childcare providers, chauffeurs, house cleaners, motivators and whatever else was needed on my behalf.

To my coworkers at Pitt County Public Health Center and the many Pitt County Government Employees – thank you for your visits, prayers and support.

Dedications

To my husband of 18 years, *Steve* – thank you for your unfailing love, strength, support and faithfulness during one of the toughest times in my life.

To my sister, *Vassie Barrett* – thank you for laying down your life for me by giving me one of your kidneys. What a priceless gift of life and love.

To my children, *Krystal, Garrison and Kevin* – you are great kids and I love you.

To my mother, *Mary* – thank you for your faith, strength and prayers through it all. You are a strong woman and I thank you for the example you have given me. You are my hero.

To my father, *Hermond* - thank you for allowing your children to grow up in church and learn about God at such an early age.

To my mother-in-law, *Rosa* - for putting your life on hold for weeks at a time to come and do whatever you could to support us through it all.

Table of Contents

Acknowledgements iii

Dedications v

Why This Book? ix

The Onion 1

The Desert 9

The Storm 17

The Grace Of God 23

God's Faithfulness 33

It Is Finished 39

Journal Entries 43

Healing Scriptures 51

Pictures 55

Why This Book?

Why did I write this book? What is different about this book? These may be some of the questions that breezed through your mind as you looked at the cover or flipped through the introductory pages; however, I encourage you to read on. I believe that you will find that this is not just another book, but yet another reason to praise and give God the glory.

This book had to be written. I have to share with as many people as possible what God did for me. What I experienced is available to countless others who desperately need to embrace the love of a compassionate Heavenly Father. I want people to know that no matter what the situation, God is able to bring you through. There is **NOTHING** too hard for God. He is so faithful, so loving, so full of grace and so full of mercy. He desires that everything you experience turn out for your good and that you come through those tough times in your life victoriously.

This is a testimony to the glory of a good God who loves you and me with an everlasting love. I have experienced the Father's love like never before and I praise Him for being a Promise Keeper, a wonderful Savior, loving Father and for being my Healer. What you will read in the next pages is but a brief account of how God carried me through the most challenging time in my life. I believe that as you read this book, you will be encouraged and challenged to trust God who "is able to do exceeding, abundantly above all that we ask or think according to the power that worketh in us." (Ephesians 3:20)

The Onion

About six years ago, I was at a bittersweet point in my life. It was as though I was given an onion and directed to eat it. Almost forcefully, I had to digest it, not just a layer at a time, but the whole fully ripened onion. As always, I wanted to do things my way, take the time to set things in place and have some control of what I was involved in. I wanted to sauté this experience, this tearjerker, this onion. Feeling somewhat consumed early on, I felt compelled to do something because there was a certain presence I had to maintain. Symbolic of onions, everyone knows that they make your eyes burn and tears begin to fall. After a while even your breath becomes unpardonable! Nevertheless, thank God for His eye salve and the sweetness of His Word that brings life and clear vision.

There were many questions that went through my mind at the onset of this bittersweet experience. Why must I eat this onion? Do I have to eat it all? Can I add some seasonings, vegetables and meat along with it so it won't be so bad? The more I thought about it, the more I was convinced, but still disillusioned, to think that I was getting ready for such a gourmet experience. Even though I saw what this big ole onion was about to bring, there was still so much denial. Against hope, I knew I had to be optimistic and trust my Heavenly Father; however, the reality was already in my face like a scrolling marquee reading, "Ready or not, here I come".

The very symptoms of my situation like the smell of onions would introduce my presence everywhere I went. I tried many times holding my breath so this onion would not get the best of me, but the more I did the more life as I had enjoyed it was suffocating me. I knew that I had but one choice to make, accept the process of peeling and cutting away what was doing me no good and allow myself to be fully cleansed … just like an onion does once inside your body. I had but one hope and dream when this journey began and that was after the cleansing, the benefits of a new "flavor" in life would begin.

As well esteemed and together as I thought I was, there were still some areas that had to be dealt with. To bring about my wholeness, one bite at a time, I had to deal with issues of pride, fear, insecurity and more pride. As they were revealed and acknowledged the work of repentance and cleansing began. God had to allow me to get to the point where He could see that I wasn't fooling myself anymore and there was no going back to the areas that lay shed and full of decay at my feet. He needed to know that He was beholding His daughter who was totally dependent on Him and ready to willingly put her trust in Him to carry her through.

In many ways, my life took on the dependencies of a child. I had a need for so many others in my life. Just like a child left to himself, my Father knew that I was chock full of it and needed a good all natural cleansing. Now, as for me, I was no different from most of you. I knew I would be obedient to my Daddy; however; I was not always exuding willingness. Nevertheless, my only choice was, once this onion was given to me, how would I eat it? Would I eat it as directed, trusting that I would not be at this table alone, or would I eat this bitterness by adding my own recipe of additives and preservatives and yet still complaining?

Though reluctantly at first, I chose to eat the onion as directed. I chose to trust God and His Word. In so doing, He showed me in the most unexpected ways that the onion I was eating would not only be my water lily but someone else's as well. Someone was going to be encouraged; someone's faith was going to be strengthened and someone who had lost hope would find that there is hope in God.

As the days stretched to weeks and the weeks to months, eventually a year and a half had passed by. God, during this time, restored me in ways that were nothing short of incredible. He showed me that I was not eating alone. There were hosts of family members (brothers and sisters in Christ) sitting at the dining table with me who were themselves in one way or another also eating. There was such etiquette and care during this eighteen-month banquet. God showed me what could really happen at the table when everyone takes their place. I was in the greatest need and the most vulnerable and it showed. Let me take you back.

Envision a little girl sitting at a table trying to eat. In most cases, she would make a mess and it was not pretty. She would eat too fast and cram in too much too soon thinking she was okay, but really she was about to choke. Someone had to be right there to help with what she had. When she had bitten off more than she could chew, there was always someone close by to help her manage just what she could handle in the right proportions.

Bernice Gorham Cherry

As you know by now, I was that little girl, and as thankful as I was for every time someone did for me what I could not do for myself, I was humbled beyond any definition I had ever known. Still dealing with areas of "I have got to get it together; I can do it", I actually felt downright crushed. People were very kind to me but I was so consumed with this physically bitter tasting experience that I could not always appreciate those who wanted to cry with me.

This was not supposed to happen to me. It did not fit with the picture of health I was supposed to be. Professionally, I coordinated an employee wellness program and at home I was definitely no hypocrite; my family was earning a degree in health education too.

During those 12 – 18 months, each day weighed it's toll. There were times when the stench of the onion became so strong that everything about me burned, my nostrils, eyes and even my pride. All I could see was tainted through the layers of stuff I did

The Onion You Are Eating Is Someone Else's Water Lily

not need. What a dark time. It was at those times that God reminded me that He was with me and that this was temporary. He was setting me up with sisters and brothers who were filling the heavens with prayers that cleared the very stench of the onion. I only needed to keep my eyes and ears focused on what the Bible had to say about my situation and believe it.

The Desert

As this journey began, I was at a stage in my life where I felt I was out in the desert all by myself. I knew that God had not left me but I felt that He had stepped back from me so that I could grow up and mature in some areas. I guess it was somewhat like a Momma Bird pushing her Baby Bird out of the nest so it can learn to fly. This was a tough time for me. I was not focused enough on God and His Word and could not clearly see what He was doing. I was finding out how dry it could be in the desert. I began to feel like I was going through the motions; I wrestled with the ability to fulfill my roles in life as wife, mother, fulltime employee and volunteer in my local church. I knew my purpose regarding these areas but knowledge alone was not enough. Not only was my physical strength slipping away but my focus was being severed literally several distinct times daily. Every immediate hope of normalcy was only briefly in view. What I did not know was that I was going to lose my ability to function in each of those areas. There was going to be a rebuilding and I was going to be vulnerable to my own redesign.

My need for others and belonging was strong but in my attempts to continue life as I enjoyed it, I found connecting difficult. Have you ever been at that point before? I'm talking about the point where you need relationship with others but just can't seem to connect. Have you ever needed someone to hear you so badly that your insides were screaming, "HELP" but the word would not come out of your mouth? It is almost painful – no, it really is painful.

The Onion You Are Eating Is Someone Else's Water Lily

I remember one night at a women's fellowship I was in a skit called "Miss Understood". In this particular skit, I played the part of "Miss Got It All Together". This character really seemed to have it all together on the outside but on the inside there was much stress and anxiety. At the end of the skit different people began to share how the skit had ministered to them. Before I knew it, I was on my feet. I began to share how the character I played suited me perfectly. I went on to say something else but never got to finish because the alarm went off in one of the adjacent buildings. By the time it was determined that everything was okay and people settled, my moment was gone and someone else had stood up to share.

Some time after that, I can remember writing a note to the Lord. In the note, I told the Lord that I wanted it easy and that I was tired of the hard way. In spite of what I wanted to hear, I knew it was Him responding, "Bernice, that is not what is best for you; in order for you to be what I have called you to be, there has to be some hardness and some trials". This was a real challenge to my faith because what I was seeing and feeling was definitely not easy and it surely was hard and a trial if I had ever known one. God had to teach me that the walk of faith into His perfect will sometimes begins on a religious road before there is confidence in knowing ones steps were ordered. It was not until later that I accepted this.

One day a dear sister in Christ shared with me a 30-day plan for reading and studying God's word in light of it's application to my life. It was really like sunshine rising early in the mornings or the dawning of the evening while everyone was gone to bed. Just being alone in God's presence through His Word was precious. I was able to read, study, and apply God's Word to my life on a daily basis. These times of solitude were strengthening me in some areas that made me feel as though I was surrendering my life to the Lord for the first time. My focus on Him was beginning to broaden.

The Onion You Are Eating Is Someone Else's Water Lily

Even though things were going great for a while, I somehow became distracted in the midst of doing all those "good" things. The feelings of lack of purpose began to creep up again. Along with that, the feeling of wanting it easy returned also. My life at this point was shaded with confusion. I felt that I was giving-giving-giving and just could not give anymore. My life was like a merry-go-round that was going around so fast that I just wanted to jump off for a while and take a break. I simply just wanted to escape and be refreshed without such complications.

A lot of what I was going through was exacerbated by my perfectionism – wanting everything to be perfect all the time. I was trying so hard to do so much, so much in my own strength. You can only go for so long doing that because eventually you get tired. Your body gets tired; your mind gets tired and even your spirit gets tired and that is where I was. I needed affirmation so badly and it seemed that it only came when there was achievement in some form. Though I did not realize it, my identity was being defined by my roles in life. In and of itself, that is not a bad thing. The problem comes when who you are in Christ becomes lost in all of it.

I was so overwhelmed that one Saturday, I got in the back of my closet, sat on the floor and closed the door. Doing that was my way of jumping off that merry-go-round and escaping to myself. I remember hearing my husband go through the house calling my name but I would not answer. I wanted a break and did not want to be found, at least not then. Needless to say, he found me and gently pulled me out of the closet. He and I talked but it was hard to fully explain where I felt I was. Nothing was clearer than the fact that I needed some time and space. Recognizing my desperate need for emotional, physical, spiritual and mental space, he decided to take the kids to the pool.

While they were gone, I put on a tape and the song that was playing was like a person talking to God asking Him to show them the way. At that point, I fell on my knees and cried out to

The Onion You Are Eating Is Someone Else's Water Lily

God from the depths of my being for help. I asked God to show me the way. I told him "I give up; I surrender. I'm tired of doing things my way and in my own strength; I want it Your Way." What a release! I believe that as I surrendered my will to His will, it opened the door for God to move in my life in a way that would lead to a strengthening of my relationship with Him. Praise God, the scales on my eyes and mirage of an oasis were being replaced with substance, but then…

The Storm

About six months after that (December 1997), I went to a dermatologist about three places in my scalp where I had lost some hair. I had actually noticed this hair loss earlier but thought the hair products I was using were causing dryness in my scalp resulting in hair loss. When I visited the dermatologist, he said that the places in my scalp looked like Discoid Lupus. It is an autoimmune disease (your body's cells begin to attack its own cells), which affects the skin.

To say the least, I was shocked. I went in thinking that he was going to tell me the hair loss was due to eczema or some other excessively dry skin condition. I was expecting to get some cream or ointment and be sent on my merry way. NOT. He performed a biopsy of one the areas to see if indeed it was lupus and a blood sample was also taken to see if my internal organs were being affected. He told me that even though it looked like lupus, not to worry about it, go on home and have a Merry Christmas.

On January 2, 1998, the results confirmed his diagnosis. This lab work came back showing severe anemia and gross inadequacies in the functioning of my kidneys. I was then referred to a rheumatologist who did further lab work which revealed that blood and protein were showing up in my urine. Another referral was made to a kidney specialist (nephrologist) who performed a biopsy of my kidney on January 29, 1998. I later learned through the nephrologist that I had been diagnosed with one of the worst cases of lupus that a person could have. He also told me that when the pathologist looked at my kidney biopsy, the only positive thing to be said was that

The Onion You Are Eating Is Someone Else's Water Lily

there was no scar tissue. My kidneys were shutting down so fast that there was no time for scars.

What a blow. Prior to this, the extent of my medical care had been a tonsillectomy when I was ten years old, annual physicals, obstetrical care during my three pregnancies and orthopedic care when I dislocated my kneecap the previous year. I did not need clinical advice on this one; I was in a state of shock and headed for depression. I could not believe this was happening to me. This was not supposed to be happening to me. After all, I'm a *good* Christian, *good* wife, *good* mother, *good* employee, and a *good* church member.

These were the thoughts that ran through my mind as I thought about the diagnosis. But then the truth about what I was thinking hit me and oh, did it hit me hard. In essence, I was thinking that this should not be happening to me because I thought I was "all that" I mentioned above. It was if subconsciously, I thought it should be happening to someone else. God really had to deal with me and my *good* self about these thoughts. As He did, I began to see how these thoughts had their root in pride. I knew what the Bible said about pride and did not want to go there. I had to line up my thoughts, actions and my words with the Word of God. As God continued to show me myself, I felt ashamed and began to ask God to forgive me and cleanse me. Thank the Lord for grace and forgiveness.

I had to remember that God did not promise us that we would not have trials in our lives or that our trials would be easy. He did promise, however, to never leave us or forsake us (Hebrews 13:5). He promised in Isaiah 43:2 that "when you pass through the waters, I will be with you; and through the rivers, they shall not overflow you. When you walk through the fire, you shall not be burned." (Isaiah 43:2) I had to accept the reality that this was something that my family and I would have to go through and the only way we were going to make it was to

The Onion You Are Eating Is Someone Else's Water Lily

put into practice the truth of God's Word. As for me, I had to bite the onion, peel and all.

The Grace Of God

Based on the severity of my case, my doctors felt that aggressive measures needed to be taken in order to arrest the lupus, restore function to my kidneys and prevent any more damage. These measures included receiving cytoxan (chemotherapy) treatments and 100mg of Prednisone per day.

On February 11, 1998, I had my first chemo treatment after which I experienced a lot of nausea, vomiting and diarrhea. Prior to the treatment, I experienced a lot of fluid retention and swelling. In fact, I gained over 20 pounds within what seemed like a matter of two weeks. The Prednisone caused some of the swelling, particularly in my face. There was fluid seemingly everywhere even in my eyes. My feet became so swollen that slits had to be cut in a pair of my shoes in order for me to wear them. I became limited in the number of clothes in my closet that I could fit in as well. This became an issue for me later on. I was not used to weighing so much and the sight of myself in the mirror was like looking at someone else.

Additional blood work was done after this treatment and it revealed that instead of my lab results showing improvement, they were worse. The only option available at this point was dialysis. My doctors felt that dialysis would help rid my body of the poisons and toxins that had built up in my system and would allow the chemotherapy treatments to be more effective. Dialysis - yet another unexpected blow. To this day, I still remember the call from the doctor. I also remember my husband and I just holding each other, and praying and crying. Everything felt so unreal. I had no symptoms other than being tired. But hey, I was working full-time trying to be a *good* employee, married trying to be a *good* wife, had three children and was trying to be a *good* mother. I thought this was normal. Who wouldn't be tired?

My appointment at the hospital's hemodialysis unit was scheduled for 1:30 pm. Upon arrival, my weight, blood pressure and temperature were taken. I was then prepped for insertion of a femoral catheter. This would be the initial access route for dialysis. I was afraid but God is so good in that He worked it out such that the assistant for this procedure was a born again Christian. She prayed with me and for me prior to and throughout my time there. And oh how I needed prayer. At one point, I was in so much pain that I actually felt like I was going to die. Several days later, I was transferred from HDU to one of the floors. While there, I had a seizure. An MRI, EKG, EEG and CAT scan were conducted after the seizure and all came back normal. Thank you, Lord! The precious thing about all of this is even in the midst of everything that was going on, I could hear the Spirit of God telling me that all this was temporary. He gave me peace and assured me that He was with me. I am reminded of Psalm 23, "yea though I walk through the valley of the shadow of death, I will fear no evil for though art with me. Thy rod and thy staff they comfort me." Oh, how I thank God for His Word.

After this discharge, I began dialysis three times per week at the local dialysis center. For me, this was a four-hour process. For a little while, things seemed to be progressing well but then I began to have elevated blood pressure readings. In April, I was transported back to the hospital via rescue squad. While at the dialysis center, my blood pressure had risen to over 200/120. This resulted in a series of seizures. Over the six days that I was in the hospital, the doctors and nurses experimented with various blood pressure medications. This was honestly a tough time for me – tough for my flesh – in that I was getting tired of the battle. Trusting God was and is not hard. His Word is true, flawless, and settled. I knew that, but lining up my flesh with the Word presented a challenge. The Lord allowed me to withstand this challenge through renewing my mind with healing scriptures. I thank God for the sister who shared these with me and for everyone that the Lord led to call me or stop by the house and share a particular scripture or song with me. I also thank God for an instrumental tape entitled "Rest". When I went to dialysis and during my time at home, I was armed with the Word of God and song.

In the meantime, dialysis continued and so did the chemotherapy once a month. Eventually my hair began to fall out and shopping for a wig became the inevitable. But even in that, God allowed my family and me to laugh. I remember when I went to buy my first wig. My husband and children, who at the time were 10, 8, and 3 years old, also went along. It was interesting trying on wigs my children selected and then watching their reactions. At one point, during my time of wig wearing a good friend of mine who is a licensed cosmetologist went out and bought me a wig. She even came to my house, cut and styled it for me. I tell you God is so good and He cares about those things that concern us. He knew I needed some help. Even though I had done my hair myself for years, when it came to choosing a wig, it was hard for me to find one that was just right.

There were times when I felt so ugly. My face was so puffy and swollen and dark that I looked like a totally different person. It got to the point that I avoided mirrors whenever possible. I gained so much weight that I went up four dress sizes. I had to give this to God. As I was praying one day, I asked God to restore my outward beauty – not so people could come up to me and say I looked good but so that God would get the glory for the wonderful thing He had done. I asked God to first give me inner beauty that would shine forth on the outside. I declared that the puffiness in my face, the hair growth on my face, the hair loss and the weight gain would pass and that in its place would be thick, healthy hair and restored facial shape, skin and whatever else this disease had taken from me.

In October, I was back in the hospital again. This time I had nine seizures one after the other. I don't remember much about this hospital visit at all because I was heavily sedated much of the time.

Shortly after this, I had surgery for insertion of a catheter into my peritoneal cavity so that I could begin doing dialysis at home. As November rolled around, I was becoming impatient. My thinking was along the lines of, *okay God, am I done with this yet? When are you going to manifest this healing you promised me? I am so tired of all of this.* I felt like I just could not fight anymore. I became angry – angry about my situation and I was angry with God. *Why wouldn't He go ahead and just do what I knew He had the power to do. How much longer would I have to wait? When was my miracle going to take place?* These were all questions that came to my mind during that time although all of them were not articulated. Realizing my anger, I confessed it to God, asked Him to forgive me and continued to wait.

Bernice Gorham Cherry

December was approaching and Christmas would soon be here. Although my body was weak, I was looking forward to going home. I was able to eat a little of my Mom's good cooking. I was so weak and felt so yucky, but it was good to be home with my family.

The Tuesday after Christmas, I was back in the hospital again for what would turn out to be a three-week stay. During that time, I was bleeding internally but the doctors did not know where the bleeding was coming from or where it was going. I was given a spinal tap, bone marrow test, aphaeresis and I do not know what all else during this admission. It was such a blessing when the doctor said that I could go home. Not only was I glad to be well enough to go home, but also glad to be able to sleep in my own bed and actually sit on my own toilet. During that admission, I was not allowed out of bed so the bedpan and I became very good friends. It is amazing what you

The Onion You Are Eating Is Someone Else's Water Lily

come to appreciate and value when you have to go for a time without it.

God's Faithfulness

Time and time again throughout the dialysis, nine hospitalizations, seizure episodes, emergency room visits, chemotherapy, blood transfusions and gall bladder surgery, God's unmerited favor was upon my life. He was ever reminding me that He loved me with an everlasting love and that He was in control. He was also showing me that he had not fallen asleep and let Satan sneak in. He let me know that I needed this trial but it was a trial that He was going to bring me through victoriously. God assured me that He was going to turn this situation around and that this was temporary. I only needed to focus on Him, stand on His promises of healing, trust and draw closer to Him.

So what did I do? I drew closer to Him through prayer, praise, worship, reading His Word and literature given to me by several of my dear sisters and brothers in Christ. I also listened to and meditated on healing scripture tapes and literature everyday. Certain scriptures were key to me during this time. Proverbs 4:20 – 22 was shared with me early on by one of our brothers from the church. This scripture says, "My son, give attention to my words; incline your ear to my sayings. Do not let them depart from your eyes; keep them in the midst of your heart; for they are life to those who find them, and health to all their flesh". From this scripture, I learned that God's prescription for my healing was partaking of His Word every day. So just as I daily took the different medicines prescribed by my doctors, I took God's medicine – His Word. Another scripture that was a blessing to me was Psalm 118:17, "I shall not die, but live, and declare the works of the Lord". That was my confession. Yet another scripture that became precious to me was Psalm 107:20. It reads, "He sent His word and healed them, and delivered them from their destructions." All of these scriptures and others helped to strengthen my faith that healing was for me. It was not because I had been good enough to merit healing, but because God is faithful to His Word. One of the many things God's Word tells us about healing is found in Isaiah 53:5 which says that because of the stripes Jesus bore, we are healed. We are told in Numbers 23:19 that we can trust that God will do what He says. This verse says, "God is not a man, that He should lie, nor the son of man that He should repent. Has He said, and will He not do? Or has He spoken, and will He not make it good?" I had to trust God when there were no symptoms and when symptoms were shouting out to me. I had to trust Him when the doctors had no good news of progress to share.

I also read the book, <u>Christ The Healer</u>, which really opened my eyes on Jesus Christ as my Healer and healing being a part of what was paid for on the cross. Through this book, I learned that even more than I needed to seek healing, I needed to seek the Healer.

I have to be honest; there were times when I was so afraid and there were so many opportunities to be afraid. Times when my mind was battling thoughts of would I or when would I have another seizure. There were also thoughts of would I be able to see my children grow up or grow old with my husband. The fears were real and yet God's Word was more real and more powerful than my fears. One day I heard someone say that thoughts entertained become imaginations and imaginations entertained become strongholds. I could not afford to entertain those fearful thoughts but had to say what the Bible said about my situation. To do that, I had to first grab hold of II Corinthians 10:4 – 5. This scripture reads, "For the weapons of our warfare are not carnal but mighty in God for pulling down strongholds, casting down arguments and every high thing that exalts itself

The Onion You Are Eating Is Someone Else's Water Lily

against the knowledge of God, bringing every thought into captivity to the obedience of Christ".

God's Word is so powerful. We are told in Hebrews 4:12 that "the word of God is living and powerful, and sharper than any two-edged sword, piercing even to the division of soul and spirit, and of joints and marrow, and is a discerner of the thoughts and intents of the heart." The more of God's word I read, meditated on and spoke out of my mouth, the more my faith was strengthened, the more I began to experience God's peace and His rest and the more I was able to see victory in my situation.

It Is Finished

Several weeks after this discharge, my sister said she wanted to be tested to see if she would be a match for a kidney transplant. In March 1999, she was tested and on April 12, 1999, I received a call from the transplant coordinator who informed me that my sister was a match. She further stated that they could do the transplant the following week. I was excited and at the same time a little scared. This would be major surgery that not only I would undergo but my sister as well. I had to give my fear to God and trust that He would do as He promised – to bring us safely through, and He did. My sister was discharged three days later and I was discharged five days

Bernice Gorham Cherry

later. Three months later, she got married and two years later she gave birth to twin boys. Oh, isn't God good?

I remember as I was lying on the couch a few days after being discharged, I began to think of what the Lord had done for me. As I thought about how He had brought me through this trial, I began to cry and I could not stop thanking Him. This was my cry of victory. I knew that this battle was finished. The onion was fully eaten and now digestion would continue to take its full course.

So what is your onion? Is it a life-threatening diagnosis, possible loss of a spouse through separation, divorce or death, or is it financial ruin? Maybe your onion is a child who has gone astray? No matter what it is, you can eat that onion. One bite at a time; you can eat it. I did and God does not love me any more than He loves you. Just like He helped me eat my onion; He will help you eat yours. I know it is not easy but it is essential that you trust Him in your current situation for He who is faithful will

The Onion You Are Eating Is Someone Else's Water Lily

never leave you. You do not have to go through this alone. Whether you are beginning to eat or are at the very center of your onion, eat it in faith that the beauty of the water lily might be seen and God might be glorified.

Journal Entries

My initial thinking regarding this trial was like *"okay God, I have prayed so turn this situation around right now so I can go on with my life".* But that was not God's plan in this trial. Accepting this as a part of God's plan was important because it meant that I was releasing control of my life and trusting Him to do what He had promised – to heal me, to never leave me, etc. I had to continue to focus on Him. One of the ways He helped me to do this was through journaling. Sometimes my journal entries were just a few sentences and sometimes they were paragraphs that never seemed to end. On the next few pages, I would like to share some of my journal entries with you. They were and continue to be a blessing to me, and I believe they will be for you as well. I encourage you to do the same. Tell God all about it and listen as he speaks peace and comfort to your soul.

2/9/98: As I looked at the cross, Jesus said, "Bernice this is for you. This is for your situation; this is for your healing. This is because I love you.

2/11/98: Lord, I want to fall in love with you. I want to be consistent. Thank you for your grace to do so.

3/24/98: On Monday, the Lord spoke something to me and it was this. "My will is to never do anything just good enough or half way. When I created the heavens and the earth and sat down and rested, I did not say it is good enough, I said it is good, meaning it is complete. In addition, you do not have to settle for a good enough healing. Believe me for complete healing." That is key. Many of us settle for little when God

The Onion You Are Eating Is Someone Else's Water Lily

wants to do so much more in us and for us. We get tired and impatient. God is so good and I can't say it enough. His steadfast love never ceases and His mercies never come to an end. I am so thankful for His faithfulness.

4/5/98: I must hold on and continue to stand on God's promises for they are sure. I am convinced that God's Word is true and that He is a God that can't and will not lie. Sometimes, in the midst of the battle our flesh becomes tired. It is during those times that we seek refuge in the Word of God and in praise and worship and in praying in the Spirit. Cast not away your confidence. You're so close to the end of the battle – don't throw in the towel.

4/6/98: Jesus is beckoning me to another level in Him.
A place where more of His power and glory is revealed
A place above this world's affections and whims
A place where to His perfect will I yield
Help me, dear Jesus, to heed to your call

Bernice Gorham Cherry

Give me grace to respond quickly

And not worry whether I fall

I want to go to another level in you

Show me the way so I can take my family too

Teach me, oh Lord, and instruct me in your way

So that I may be accountable on that great day

God allows trials but as in the case of Job, He sets limits. He knows our frame and our level in Him and therefore what our limits are. In our trials, we must trust that He is in control and allow Him to win the battle and to overcome through us. When God allows a trial, it is for our good, not for our harm or for our failure.

4/16/98: Keeping my focus on Jesus – on the cross – that is my daily goal. With my eyes on the cross, I see only victory. I see only healing; I see wholeness. I don't see symptoms. With my eyes on the cross, I see the price Jesus paid for me. I see His body that was bruised and beaten for my healing. I see His blood that was shed for my sins.

Forgive me, Lord, for trying to do things in my own strength. Forgive me for trying to do things and be perfect in every way. I yield to you, Lord, and to your way. Give me your grace, Lord, to hear from you and obey. I want to hear you clearly with no distractions.

4/21/98: Trusting and yielding all of my life to God, that is what I need to do. Trust Him completely. Trust that as He promised, he will care for my every need. He will not leave me alone but will be with me every step of the way. You know our walk with God would be so easy if we'd only take God at His word. Believe that if He said it, we can believe it and be assured that as He promised, He will deliver. God is so good to me and He has always been good to me and oh so faithful.

Bernice Gorham Cherry

4/22/98: In so many ways God is speaking to me/us in the midst of this trial/storm. Reminding us of His love, reminding us of His faithfulness and reminding me that it is my choice how I go through this trial. I have a choice. I can either believe God's Word or believe the lying vanities of my flesh and the lies of the enemy. I choose to believe God and His promises – that He has delivered me; He has healed me and that He has broken the chains that have bound me.

4/24/98: This trial has nothing to do with God's displeasure with my life or with some terrible sin I have committed. Though there are areas in my life needing refinement, there is a higher purpose to all of this - a purpose that is only for my good.

4/25/98: I had dialysis today and the enemy again launched his attack with regard to my blood pressure level. As always, God was faithful. He's always there when you need Him whether he speaks a word to you directly or speaks through one of His servants. Through one of the nurses, He told me to rest and He

The Onion You Are Eating Is Someone Else's Water Lily

assured me that He was in control. After lunch, my husband and I came upstairs and prayed. We know that God is calling us to a higher place of Christian living as individuals and as husband and wife and as a family. God is telling us to prioritize and do those things that are important. God reminded us that this was a spiritual battle, the storm was passing over, the devil was defeated and He was exalted.

Healing Scriptures

Listed below are scriptures that relate to God's promises about healing. These scriptures have been a blessing to me and I know they will bless you and strengthen your faith. Read and meditate on them daily for as it says in Proverbs 4:20 –22 "they are life unto those that find them, and health to all their flesh".

But he was wounded for our transgressions, he was bruised for our iniquities: the chastisement of our peace was upon him; and with His stripes, we are healed. **Isaiah 53:5**

Bernice Gorham Cherry

Who his own self bare our sins in his own body on the tree, that we, being dead to sins, should live unto righteousness: by whose stripes ye were healed. **I Peter 2:24**

He sent His word, and healed them, and delivered them from their destructions. **Psalm 107:20**

Bless the Lord, O my soul, and forget not all His benefits: who forgiveth all thine iniquities; who healeth all thy diseases. **Psalm 103:2,3**.

O Lord my God, I cried unto thee, and thou hast healed me. **Psalm 30:2**

What time I am afraid, I will trust in you. **Psalm 56:3**

He giveth power to the faint; and to them that have no might he increaseth strength. **Isaiah 40:29**

Therefore I say unto you, what things soever ye desire, when you pray, believe that you receive them, and ye shall have them. **Mark 11:24**

God is not a man, that he should lie; neither the son of man, that he should repent: hath he said, and shall he not do it? Or hath he spoken, and shall he not make it good? **Numbers 23:19**

For the weapons of our warfare are not carnal, but might through God to the pulling down of strong holds: Casting down imagination, and every high thing that exalteth itself against the knowledge of God, and bringing into captivity every thought to the obedience of Christ **II Corinthians 10:4,5**

For the word of God is quick, and powerful, and sharper than any twoedged sword, piercing even to the dividing asunder of soul and spirit, and of the joints and marrow, and is a discerner of the thoughts and intents of the heart. **Hebrews 4:12**

Now unto him that is able to do exceeding abundantly above all that we ask or think, according to the power that worketh in us. **Ephesians 3:20**

When thou passest through the water, I will be with thee; and through the rivers, they shall not overflow thee: when thou walkest through the fire, thou shalt not be burned; neither shall the flame kindle upon thee. **Isaiah 43:2**

Pictures

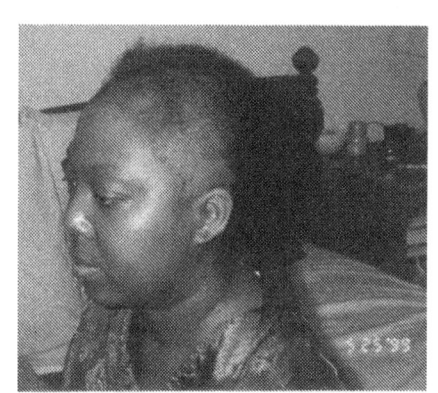

At the time of this photo, chemotherapy had taken it's effects.

As you can see, God is a restorer.
Photo by Charles Pittman.

About the Author

Bernice Cherry grew up in the small North Carolina town of Roxobel and is one of four children born to Hermond and Mary Gorham. Upon graduation from Bertie High School, she furthered her education at East Carolina University where she earned a Bachelor of Science Degree in School and Community Health Education. For the next ten years, she worked in the public health arena as a Public Health Educator. She now lives in Greenville, North Carolina with her husband and three children. "The Onion You Are Eating Is Someone Else's Water Lily" is her first book.

CPSIA information can be obtained
at www.ICGtesting.com
Printed in the USA
BVHW072219040122
625216BV00002B/286

9 781414 036205